Incentive Pieces for Guitar Students

Ralph Louis Scicchitano

iUniverse

INCENTIVE PIECES FOR GUITAR STUDENTS
A PROGRESSIVE COLLECTION OF FUN SHORT SOLOS
AND DUETS FOR FINGER-STYLE GUITAR.

iUniverse books may be ordered through booksellers or by contacting:

iUniverse
1663 Liberty Drive
Bloomington, IN 47403
www.iuniverse.com
1-800-Authors (1-800-288-4677)

Author Credits: Anytime Publications

ISBN: 978-1-5320-9928-1 (sc)
ISBN: 978-1-5320-9929-8 (e)

Library of Congress Control Number: 2020907073

Print information available on the last page.

iUniverse rev. date: 04/29/2020

PREFACE

Incentive Pieces for Guitar Students is a collection of solos and duets arranged to make fingerstyle guitar fun and interesting.

Before starting, you should have some prior experience with translating musical notation to the guitar. In the area of technique, all four fingers of the left hand should be equally developed. Sometimes students will favor the stronger index and middle fingers and over use them. However, it is important for all fingers to be trained for coordination and dexterity.

Fingerstyle or fingerpicking is when the strings are plucked with the fingers of the right hand instead of a plastic pick. Ideally, the fingertips should make string contact with a combination of flesh and nail at the same time. This is why the fingernails of the right hand should be kept a little long, filed and finished for a clean sound and smooth contact.

We will be learning fingerstyle solos instead of just learning right hand patterns for chord accompaniment. In this collection we will be concerned mostly with coordinating the melody with bass and harmonized melody with bass accompaniment. Melody is usually written with the note stems up and played on the first three strings using the index, middle and ring fingers of the right hand. However, sometimes the melody is in the bass. The bass and harmony for the melody is written with the note stems down.

Follow the suggested fingering for the left and right hands. The numbers 1, 2, 3, 4 signify left hand fingers (pointer, middle, ring and pinkie). The letters t, i, m, r signify fingers of the right hand (thumb, index, middle and ring). Many traditional systems refer to the right hand fingers with the first letters of their Spanish names (p, i, m, a). A good general right hand format is to use the thumb on the sixth, fifth and fourth string, the index finger on the third string, the middle finger on the second string and the ring finger on the first string. This format is especially useful for arpeggio (chord) passages. There will be special right hand fingering for certain situations, follow them closely to insure good right hand technique development.

Roman numerals mark fret bars and (or) position. This is the fret where the first finger of the left hand falls.

This work is dedicated to my students, whose inspiration and enthusiasms have been the impetus of its creation.

TABLE OF CONTENTS

CHRISTMAS MUSIC

INTERVAL STUDIES

ADVANCED STUDIES

[1] "CARULLI PRELUDE IN G"

FERDINANDO CARULLI 1770 - 1841
arr. R.L. Scicchitano

1

[2] "NICK'S BLUES"

R.L. Scicchitano

[3] "THE BICYCLING SONG"

R.L. Scicchitano

[4] "TIME"

R.L. Scicchitano

[5] "CLIMBING"

R. L. Scicchitano

[6] "SARA'S SONG"

R.L. Scicchitano

4

[7] "FOREST RAIN"

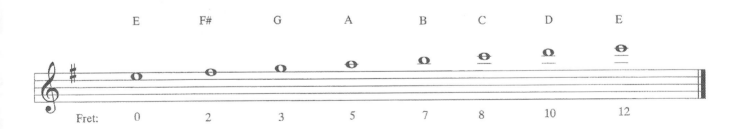

This piece is an excellent lesson for coordinating the higher notes of the first string with open string bass and open string accompaniment. Pay close attention to the right and left hand fingering. When you are ready, use the rest stroke on the first string melody. That is when you rest the (a) finger on the second string after hitting the first string. This technique is performed in one movement and will give the melody a more predominate identity.

[8] "APPALACHIAN LULLABYE"
Guitar Duet

R.L. Scicchitano

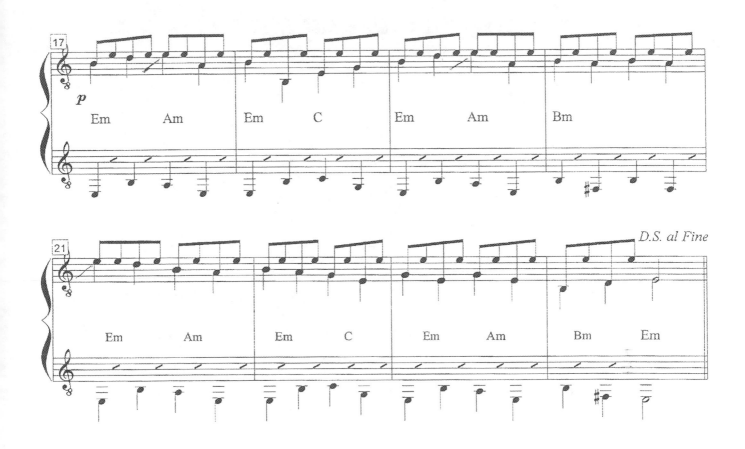

[9] "MEDIEVAL DREAM"

R.L. Scicchitano

[10] "MANUEL'S WALTZ"

R.L. Scicchitano

[11] "AN AUGUST NIGHT"

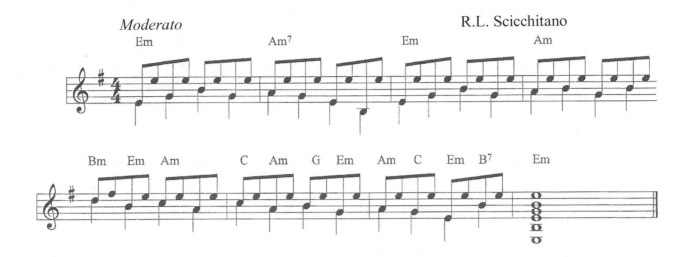

[12] "ODE TO JOY"

[13] "SUNDANCE"

SUNDANCE makes use of position changes. The piece starts out in I position, but take note of the position changes and fingering in the fourth, sixth, seventh and eighth measure. For more information on position playing see the authors book: POSITION PRIMER FOR THE GUITAR STUDENT.

[14] "MUSICAL REFLECTIONS DUET"

R.L. Scicchitano

[15] "GEORG'S BLUES"

Slow Blues

GEORG'S BLUES uses basic root bass. Do not let the bass over power the melody. In measures 13 and 14 hold your fingers down when moving from B7 bar to C bar and back to B7 bar. Roman numerals signify fret bars.

[16] "THE JOURNEY"

An exercise for the right hand

R.L. Scicchitano

[17] "CELTIC DANCE"

Allegro

R.L. Scicchitano

[18] "LADIES OF THE ICE DUET"

Allegro Moderato   *R.L. Scicchitano*

[19] "MERLIN'S DREAM"

Rubato - Moderato   R.L. Scicchitano

MERLIN'S DREAM is to be played with a *Rubato* feel. The HARVARD DICTIONARY OF MUSIC defines this as; "An elastic, flexible tempo involving slight accelerandos and ritardandos that alternate according to the requirements of musical expression."

Pay close attention to position markings and left hand fingering.

[20] "HOPE"

[21] "THE GRENCH"

Allegro   R.L. Scicchitono

[22] "THE MEDALIST"

R.L. Scicchitano

[23] "AMAZING GRACE"

John Newton
Arranged by R.L. Scicchitano

CHRISTMAS MUSIC

[24] "HARK! THE HERALD ANGELS SING"

moderato

Felix Mendelssohn
Arranged by R.L. Scicchitano

[25] "JINGLE BELLS"

Alternate the fingers of the right hand when playing the melody (stems up).
Avoid using the same finger twice in succession. Lead off with the (i) finger
on the third string.

Moderato   Arranged by R.L. Scicchitano

[26] "JOY TO THE WORLD"

triumphantly

G.F. Handel
Arranged by R.L. Scicchitano

[27] "WE WISH YOU A MERRY CHRISTMAS

allegro

Arranged by R.L. Scicchitano

Follow the tempo, dynamic and accent markings for a more expressive musical experience. Poco accelerando means to increase the speed a little. Marcato is to play marked and stressed. Ritardando is a gradual reduction in speed.

[28] "WHAT CHILD IS THIS"
(Greensleeves)

andante   Arranged by R.L. Scicchitano

26

[29] "SILENT NIGHT"

This solo can be performed with a pick or finger style.

Franze Gruber
Arranged by R.L. Scicchitano

[30] "WE THREE KINGS"

Moderato

John H. Hopkins
Arranged by R.L. Scicchitano

[31] "GOD REST YE MERRY GENTLEMEN"

Moderato

Arranged by R.L. Scicchitano

[32] "DECK THE HALLS"

Joyfully

Arranged by R.L. Scicchitano

[33] "O COME, ALL YE FAITHFUL"

INTERVAL STUDIES

STUDY IN 3rds ON THE FIRST AND SECOND STRINGS

Key of [D]

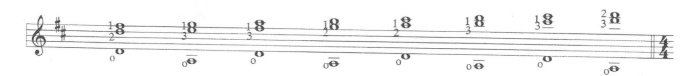

[34] "FLIGHT OF THE BUTTERFLY"

use the exact fingering as the above scale

Allegro   R.L. Scicchitano

STUDY IN 3rds ON THE SECOND AND THIRD STRINGS

Key of [A]

[35] "THE ROSE OF LOREDO"

Andante

R.L. Scicchitano

STUDY IN 3rds ON THE THIRD AND FOURTH STRINGS

Key of [E]

[36] "AMAZON NIGHT"

soft latin   R.L. Scicchitano

STUDY IN 3rds ON THE FIFTH AND SIXTH STRINGS

Key of [G]

[37] "A WARM CELLO"

Andante

R.L. Scicchitano

STUDY IN 6ths ON THE FIRST AND THIRD STRINGS

Key of [F]

Practice these intervals using the thumb (t) and ring (r) finger and the index (i) and ring finger of the right hand.

[38] "HOP, SKIP AND DROP"

Allegro

R.L. Scicchitano

mf

STUDY IN 6ths ON THE SECOND and FOURTH STRINGS

Key of [C]

[39] "BROTHER JOHN"

The offbeat (e) is open throughout.

Moderato   Arranged by R.L. Scicchitano

mf

This intervalic scale form and the one on the previous page are extremely useful for improvising leads and fills. Especially in country music.

STUDY IN 6ths ON THE THIRD AND FIFTH STRINGS

Key of [C]

[40] "CARAVAN JOURNEY"

The offbeat (e) is open throughout

Moderate   R.L. Scicchitano

mf

For a special effect try a muffled bass. This is performed with the right side of the palm resting on the strings close to the bridge. This piece can also be played in first position.

STUDY IN 6ths ON THE FOURTH AND SIXTH STRINGS

Key of [G]

[41] "SEARCHING FOR THE OASIS"

The off beat (b) is open throughout.

Moderato   R.L. Scicchitano

mf

STUDY IN 8va

Key of [C]

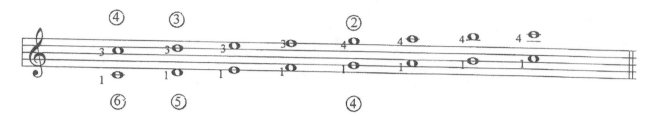

Circled numbers are string numbers.

[42] "CALYPSO"

Strike both notes with the down stroke (t). Deaden the open string with the left hand (i).

con anima   R. L. Scicchitano

STUDY IN 8va

Key of [G]

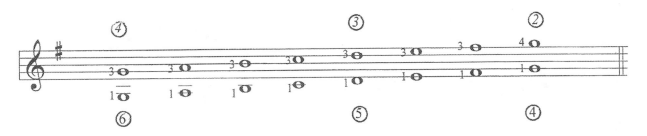

Circled numbers are string numbers.

[43] "ISLAND HOLIDAY"

Latin   R.L. Scicchitano

STUDY IN 8va

Key of [Gm]

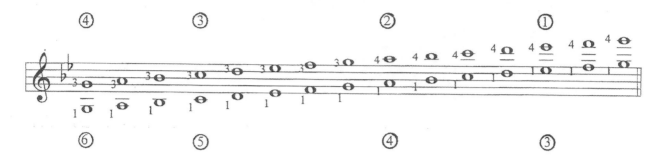

Circled numbers are string numbers.

[44] "CRAWDAD BLUES"

Slow dixie land   R.L. Scicchitano

STUDY IN 10ths (8va + 3rd)

Key of [C]

[45] "TRIO'S TUNE"

Andante   R.L. Scicchitano

STUDY IN 10ths

Key of [Em]

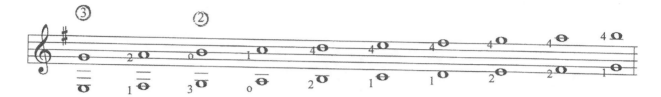

Circled numbers are the top note string number.

[46] "THE FIRETHORNE"

Andante

R.L. Scicchitano

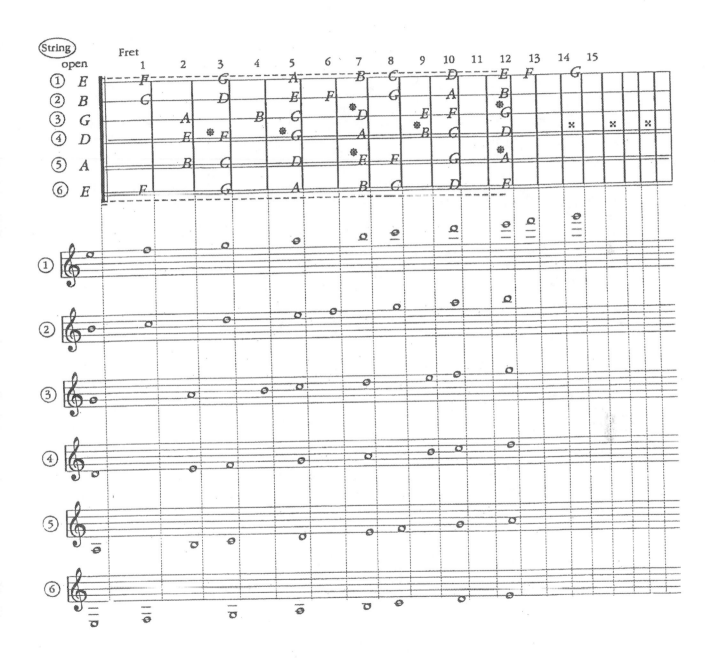

ADVANCED STUDIES

[47] "VULCAN DANCE"

From the cassette album **RALPH LOUIS ANYTIME, ANYWHERE**

[48] "GOIN' FISHIN"

From the cassette album RALPH LOUIS ANYTIME, ANYWHERE

Medium swing

R.L. Scicchitano

fade on the last time

[49] "DELTAN DANCE"

[50] "THE BEAR"

From the cassette album **RALPH LOUIS ANYTIME, ANYWHERE**

Country Rock

R. L. Scicchitano

Position Primer
FOR THE GUITAR STUDENT

An easy, fun, systematic approach to learning the fingerboard, technique, chords, moveable scale forms, keys and improvising.

RALPH LOUIS SCICCHITANO

Almost Everything
About Guitar Chords

A fun, systematic, constructive, informative
approach to the study of chords.

Ralph Louis Scicchitano

Ralph L. Scicchitano

<u>Position Primer For The Guitar Student</u>
Command of movable scale forms is pertinent to mastering the fingerboard and keys.

<u>Almost Everything about Guitar Chords</u>
An organized study of chord construction, movement, function and progression.

<u>The Eclectic Guitarist</u>
A modern approach to the development of reading and improvising skills in Jazz, Classical, Acoustic Finger-style, and Blue Grass music.

Printed in the United States
By Bookmasters